Backyard
Bugs
& Creepy-
Crawlies

I0201581

Caterpillars

Lisa Bodmorow

Explore other books at:
WWW.ENGAGEBOOKS.COM

VANCOUVER, B.C.

ℓ→ WWW.ENGAGEBOOKS.COM

Caterpillars: Level Pre-1
Backyard Bugs & Creepy Crawlies
Podmorow, Ava 2004 –
Text © 2022 Engage Books
Design © 2022 Engage Books

Edited by: A.R. Roumanis
and Sarah Harvey

Text set in Epilogue

FIRST EDITION / FIRST PRINTING

LIBRARY AND ARCHIVES CANADA CATALOGUING IN PUBLICATION

Title: Caterpillars / Ava Podmorow.
Names: Podmorow, Ava, author.
Description: Series statement: Backyard bugs & creepy-crawlies
Engaging readers: level pre-1, beginner.

Identifiers: Canadiana (print) 20220403538 | Canadiana (ebook) 20220403546
ISBN 978-177476-728-3 (hardcover)
ISBN 978-177476-729-0 (softcover)
ISBN 978-177476-730-6 (epub)
ISBN 978-177476-731-3 (pdf)

Subjects:
LCSH: Caterpillars—Juvenile literature.

Classification: LCC QL544.2 .P63 2022 | DDC J595.7813/92—DC23

This project has been made possible in part
by the Government of Canada.

Canada

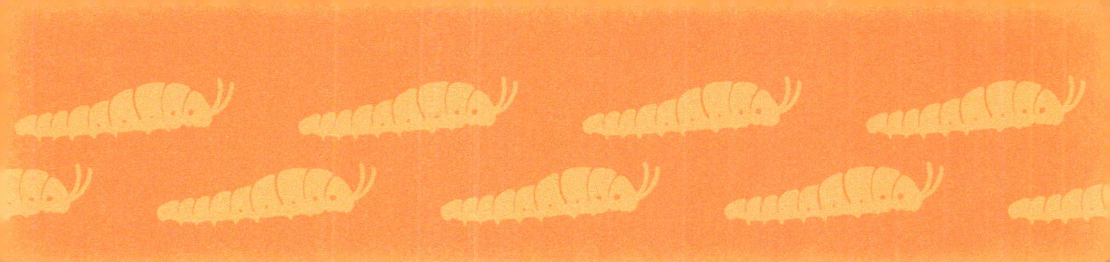

Caterpillars are always hungry!

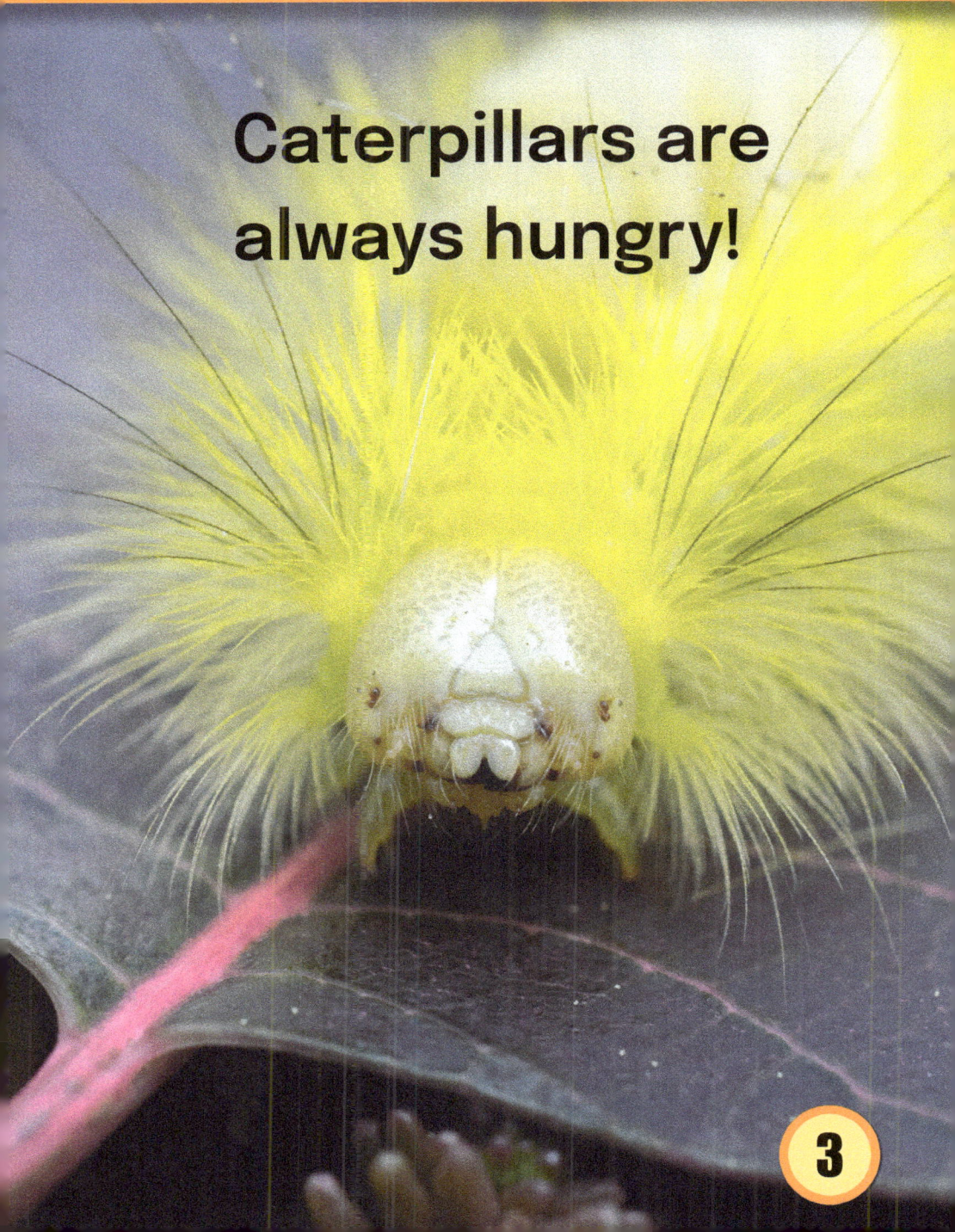

Caterpillars hatch from eggs.

They live for about two weeks.

Then they turn into butterflies or moths.

Caterpillars usually eat their own eggshells after they hatch.

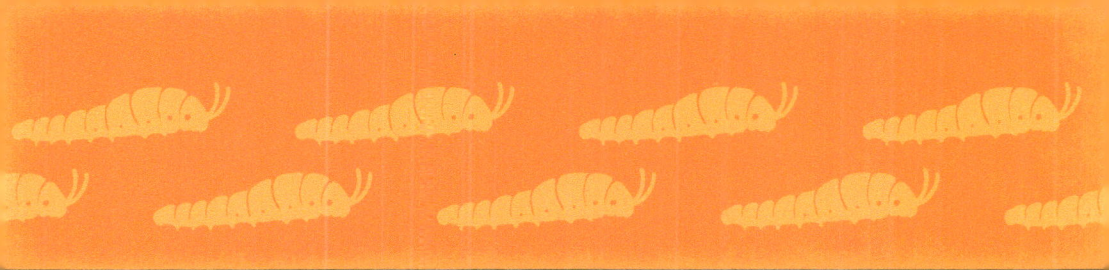

7

The only job of a
caterpillar is to eat
a lot of food.

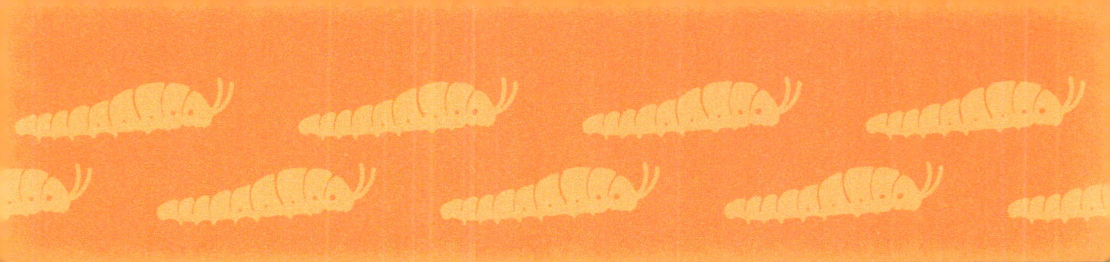

They use this food
to grow wings.

Leaves are a caterpillar's favorite food.

They also eat grass, seeds, and flowers.

Caterpillars can be many different colors.

They are usually green, brown, orange, yellow or black.

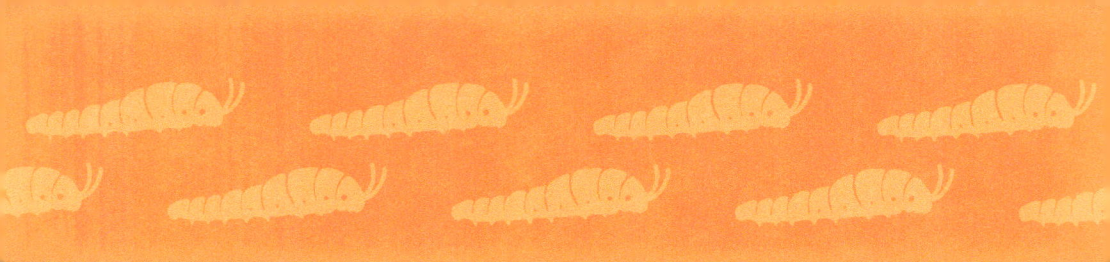

Caterpillars are very good at hiding.

They can blend in with things around them.

Caterpillars are not able to see very well.

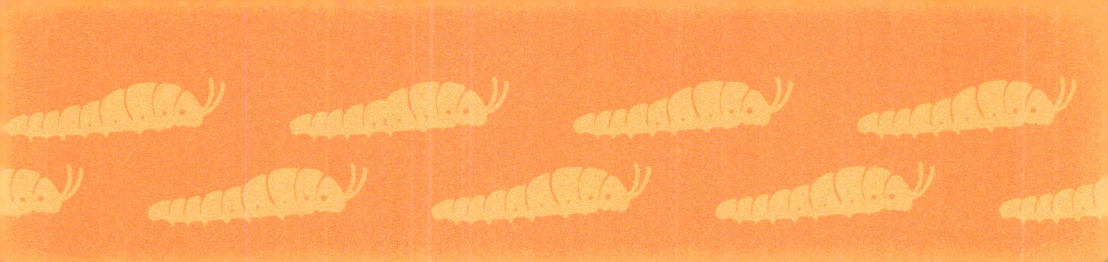

Their antennae help them get around.

Antennae

Caterpillars have six legs near their heads.

Legs

18

Prolegs help caterpillars hold onto things.

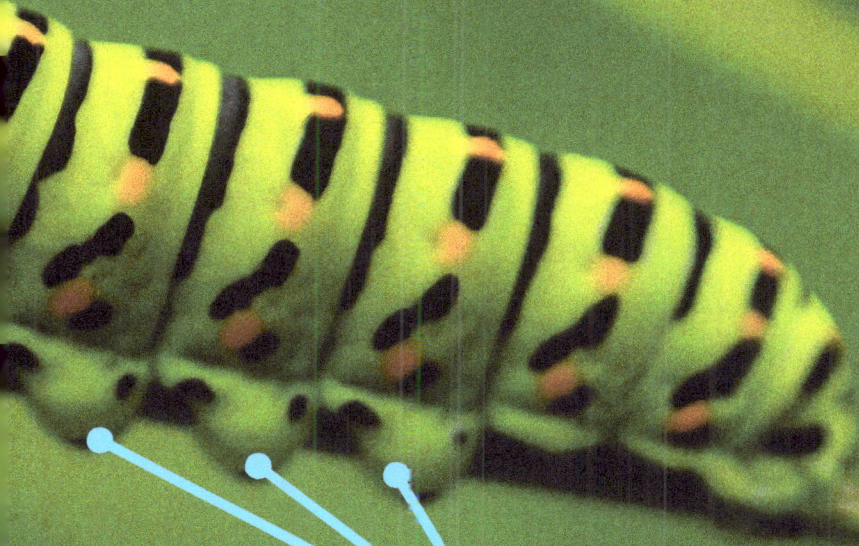

Prolegs

Caterpillars have 4,000 muscles in their bodies.

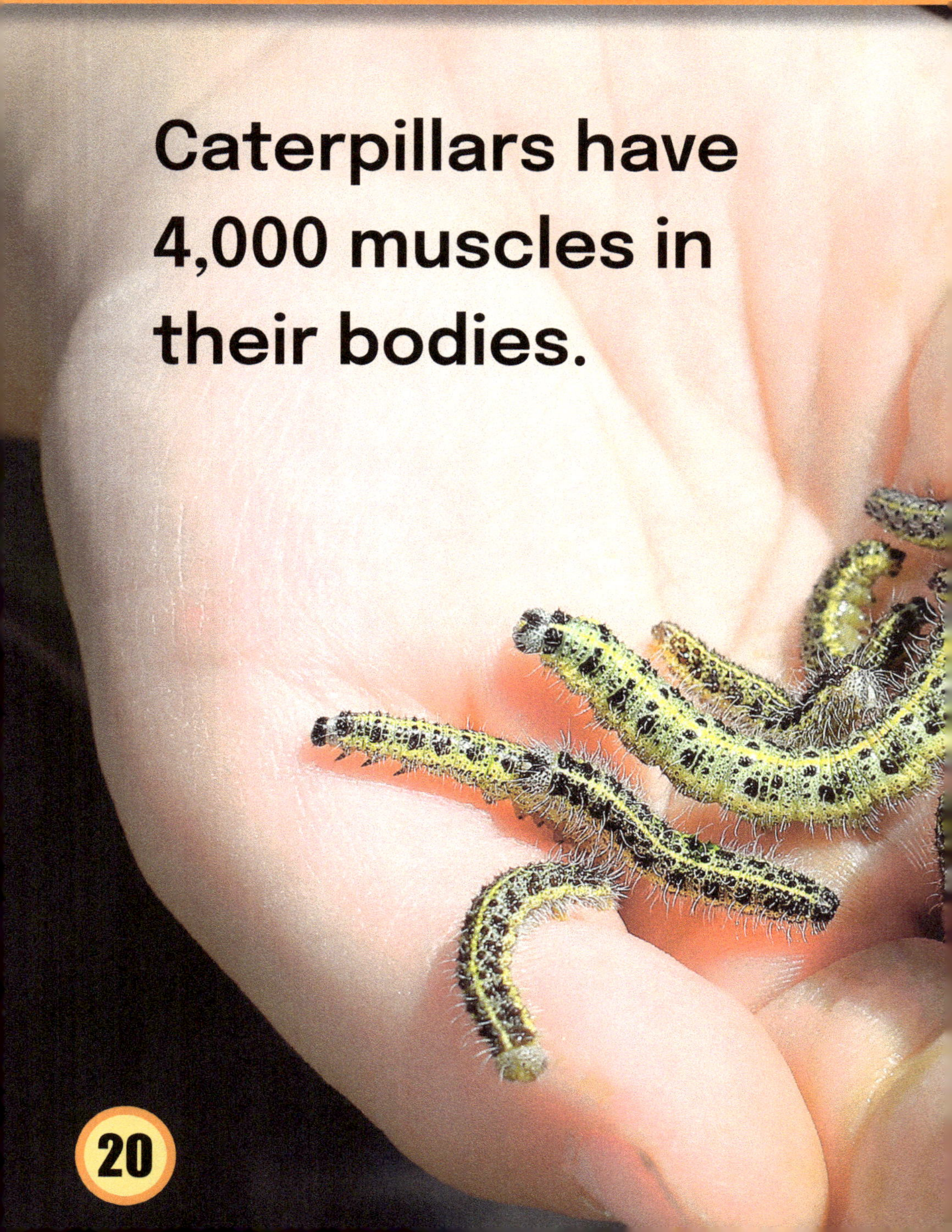

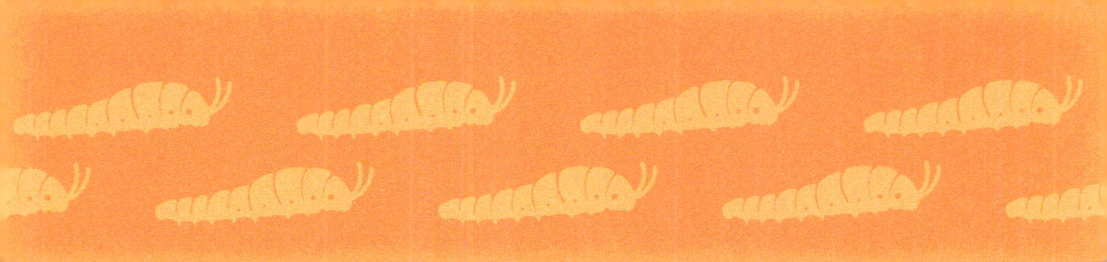

That is about six times as many as humans have!

Caterpillars do not move quickly.

They just inch along.

Caterpillars must shed their skin in order to grow.

Skin

Caterpillars make silk in their mouths.

They weave cocoons from the silk.

Then they wait to be moths or butterflies.

27

Yes, I really am a very hungry caterpillar!

29

Explore other books in the Backyard Bugs & Creepy Crawlies series!

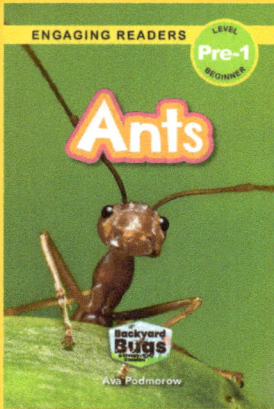

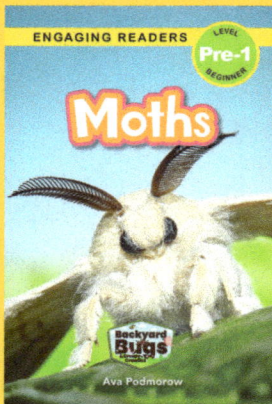

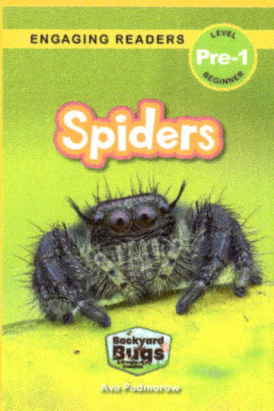

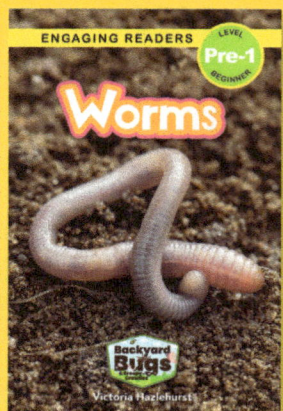

ENGAGING READERS — LEVEL Pre-1 BEGINNER
Ants
Backyard Bugs
Ava Podmorow

ENGAGING READERS — LEVEL Pre-1 BEGINNER
Beetles
Backyard Bugs
Victoria Hazlehurst

ENGAGING READERS — LEVEL Pre-1 BEGINNER
Caterpillars
Backyard Bugs
Ava Podmorow

ENGAGING READERS — LEVEL Pre-1 BEGINNER
Grasshoppers
Backyard Bugs
Ava Podmorow

ENGAGING READERS — LEVEL Pre-1 BEGINNER
Moths
Backyard Bugs
Ava Podmorow

ENGAGING READERS — LEVEL Pre-1 BEGINNER
Snails
Backyard Bugs
Ava Podmorow

ENGAGING READERS — LEVEL Pre-1 BEGINNER
Spiders
Backyard Bugs
Ava Podmorow

ENGAGING READERS — LEVEL Pre-1 BEGINNER
Wasps
Backyard Bugs
Sarah Harvey

ENGAGING READERS — LEVEL Pre-1 BEGINNER
Worms
Backyard Bugs
Victoria Hazlehurst

Visit www.engagebooks.com/readers

Explore books in the Animals In The City series.

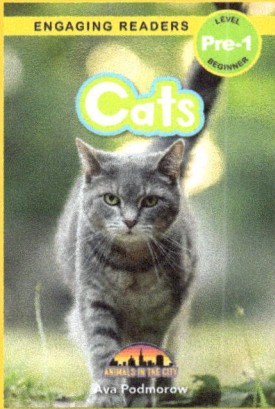

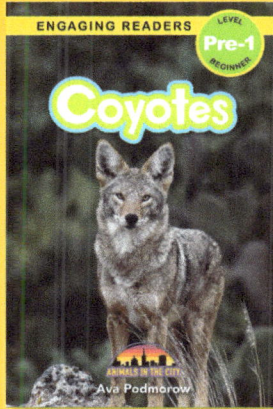

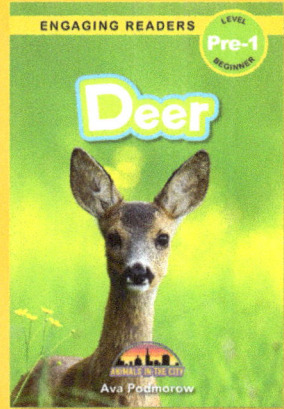

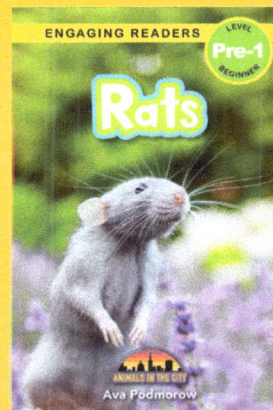

ENGAGING READERS — LEVEL Pre-1 BEGINNER
Cats
Ava Podmorow

ENGAGING READERS — LEVEL Pre-1 BEGINNER
Coyotes
Ava Podmorow

ENGAGING READERS — LEVEL Pre-1 BEGINNER
Deer
Ava Podmorow

ENGAGING READERS — LEVEL Pre-1 BEGINNER
Owls
Ava Podmorow

ENGAGING READERS — LEVEL Pre-1 BEGINNER
Pigeons
Ava Podmorow

ENGAGING READERS — LEVEL Pre-1 BEGINNER
Rabbits
Ava Podmorow

ENGAGING READERS — LEVEL Pre-1 BEGINNER
Raccoons
Sarah Harvey

ENGAGING READERS — LEVEL Pre-1 BEGINNER
Rats
Ava Podmorow

ENGAGING READERS — LEVEL Pre-1 BEGINNER
Skunks
Ava Podmorow

Visit www.engagebooks.com/readers